Listening Advantage

4

Tom Kenny
Tamami Wada

HEINLE
CENGAGE Learning™

Australia • Brazil • Japan • Korea • Mexico • Singapore • Spain • United Kingdom • United States

D0102647

Listening Advantage, Student Book 4
Kenny / Wada

Publisher: Andrew Robinson
Executive Editor: Sean Bermingham
Senior Development Editor: Derek Mackrell
Assistant Editor: Sarah Tan
Director of Global Marketing: Ian Martin
Content Project Manager: Tan Jin Hock
Senior Print Buyer: Mary Beth Hennebury
Illustrator: Edwin Ng
Cover/Text Designer/Compositor: C. Hanzie / M. Chong @ CHROME Media Pte. Ltd.
Cover Images: CHROME Media Pte. Ltd. / Photodisc, Inc.

Photo Credits
Photos.com: page 7 (top right); iStockphoto: pages 7 (second row left and bottom three), 8 (top), 12 (bottom row all except center right), 13, 16 (bottom row center left), 20 (top row far right), 42, 44, 47, 68; Shutterstock: pages 8 (bottom row all), 12 (top and bottom row center right), 16 (all except bottom row center left), 20 (all except top row far right), 23, 24, 25, 31, 32, 33, 38, 46, 55, 56, 58, 62, 63, 69, 73

The authors and publisher would like to thank the following reviewers for their help during the development of this series:
Mike Bryan, Nihon University Junior/Senior High School; **David Buchanan**, St. Dominic High School; **Hsin-Hwa Chen**, Yuan Ze University; **Wong Fook Fei**, Universiti Kebangsaan; **Ding Guocheng**, Shanghai Jincai Middle School; **Caroline C. Hwang**, National Taipei University of Technology; **Michelle Misook Kim**, Kyung Hee University; **Young Hee Cheri Lee**, Reading Town USA English Language Institute; **Hae Chin Moon**, Korea University; **Chieko Okada**, Toho Senior High School; **Hiromi Okamura**, Toho Senior High School; **Kate Mastruserio Reynolds**, University of Wisconsin - Eau Claire; **Yoshi Sato**, Nagoya University of Foreign Studies; **Joe Spear**, Hanbat National University; **Keiko Takahashi**, Ikeda Senior High School; **Yanan Une-aree**, Bangkok University; **Mei-ling Wu**, Mackay Medicine, Nursing and Management College; the students and teachers of Nagoya High School

Student Book ISBN-13: 978-1-4240-0251-1
Student Book ISBN-10: 1-4240-0251-6
Student Book + Student CD-ROM ISBN-13: 978-1-4240-0244-3
Student Book + Student CD-ROM ISBN-10: 1-4240-0244-3

Heinle
20 Channel Center Street
Boston, Massachusetts 02210
USA

Cengage Learning is a leading provider of customized learning solutions with office locations around the globe, including Singapore, the United Kingdom, Australia, Mexico, Brazil, and Japan. Locate our local office at:
international.cengage.com/region

Cengage Learning products are represented in Canada by Nelson Education, Ltd.

Visit Heinle online at **elt.heinle.com**
Visit our corporate website at **www.cengage.com**

Printed in Canada
1 2 3 4 5 6 7 8 9 10   12 11 10 09

Contents

Scope and Sequence

Daily Life

Unit	Lesson	Language/Strategy	Catch It!
1 Learning a Language *Page 8*	A Why learn English? B I don't think it's so hard.	• Stating conditions • Giving opinions	Listening for negatives
2 Education for Life *Page 12*	A Sure, why not? B. What do you mean?	• Hedging approval • Asking for explanation	Listening for consonants
3 Attitudes Toward Work *Page 16*	A I just want to let you know. B It sounds like a good deal.	• Softening in formal situations • Making a summary comment	Contrastive stress

Fun and Leisure

Unit	Lesson	Language/Strategy	Catch It!
4 Hobbies *Page 20*	A I'd love to, but . . . B Uh . . . what do you call it?	• Refusing politely • Showing that you're searching for a word	Homophones
5 Reading *Page 24*	A Be certain to come prepared! B It was a great book!	• Pointing out information • Guessing the word	Voiced and voiceless consonants
6 Consumerism *Page 28*	A Buying is believing! B Shopping is entertainment!	• Interrupting politely • Showing that you're thinking	Missing sounds

People

Unit	Lesson	Language/Strategy	Catch It!
7 Ideal Partner *Page 38*	**A** Fortunately, they both have great jobs! **B** Our growth as a couple	• Emphasizing an attitude • Restating the main point	Reconstructing ellipses
8 Co-workers *Page 42*	**A** There's no reason to quit. **B** Let's hear some ideas.	• Dissuading • Reacting with encouragement	*Wh-* and *how* questions
9 Historic Figures *Page 46*	**A** He was a real genius! **B** Modern heroes	• Asking permission • General extenders	Diphthong pronunciation

The Future

Unit	Lesson	Language/Strategy	Catch It!
10 Globalization *Page 50*	**A** The world's getting smaller! **B** The rich get richer . . .	• Contrasting • Holding the floor	Intrusion
11 Earth's Resources *Page 54*	**A** It's a major concern. **B** We're running out!	• Prefacing concerns • Tripling your reaction	Distinguishing vowels
12 Discovery *Page 58*	**A** Solutions to global problems **B** Welcome to the future!	• Emphasizing • Changing the word	Reported speech

Introduction

Listening in a foreign language is sometimes very difficult. People talk very fast and they use a lot of words and difficult language. *Listening Advantage* **will help you!**

Real situations and interesting topics

Listening Advantage uses situations from real life:

People in *Listening Advantage* talk about interesting things:

Useful language and pronunciation practice

Language Focus will teach you useful language from real life.

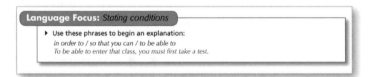

Catch It! will help you understand the way that English speakers talk.

Important strategies

Conversation Strategy sections show you how to listen more actively.

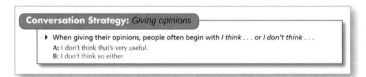

Practice your strategies in the *Talk It Over* and *Try It Out!* sections.

Test taking skills

The *Self-Study* section and *Practice Tests* give lots of listening test practice.

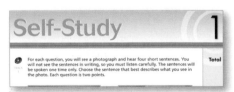

To become a good listener, listen as much as you can—in class and outside class. We hope you enjoy using *Listening Advantage***! Good luck!**

Tom and Tamami

Useful Expressions

Excuse me, I have a question.

I'm not sure I understand.

Is this right?

What did you get for number 1?

Could you say that again, please?

Could you speak more slowly, please?

Hold on. Let me think . . .

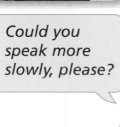

Learning a Language

Lesson A — Why learn English?

Warm-up

 A Draw lines to match the vocabulary items in blue on the left with their correct meaning on the right. Listen and check.

1	study formally	**a**	enough
2	requirement	**b**	very
3	enroll in a class	**c**	top goal
4	all the incentive I need	**d**	in a classroom
5	studying hard is my first priority	**e**	something you need
6	I'll be straight with you	**f**	honest
7	a good opportunity	**g**	temporarily, for now
8	exceptionally useful	**h**	join
9	just in the meantime	**i**	chance
10	have sufficient vocabulary	**j**	reason

B For you, what is the most difficult thing about learning English? Discuss with a partner.

Listening

 A Four speakers are talking about why they study another language. Listen for where each speaker is from. Number the places **1–4**. On the line below each photo, write what language the speaker wants to learn.

a ☐ _____   b ☐ _____   c ☐ _____   d ☐ _____

B Listen again. What is each speaker's reason for studying another language? Circle **a** or **b**.

❶ **a** for work
    b for school

❷ **a** for school
    b for travel

❸ **a** for work
    b for pleasure

❹ **a** for travel
    b for school

Further Listening

 A Four people plan to study at a private English school. What is their greatest concern about enrolling at the school? Listen and number their concerns 1–4 in the order you hear them.

a Scheduling of classes _____
b Size of class _____
c Cost of lessons _____
d Choice of textbook _____

 B Listen again. What is implied in each of the conversations? Circle the best answer.

1 a The customer wants one-on-one communication with the teacher.
   b The manager is annoyed by the customer's questions.
2 a The customer's favorite color is gold.
   b The manager will put her in another class until the one she wants is available.
3 a The manager will give a discount only to high-fluency students.
   b The customer prefers online classes to regular classes.
4 a The customer is not really a good student.
   b The manager will try to find a class that suits the student's schedule.

Language Focus: *Stating conditions*

▸ Use these phrases to begin an explanation:
in order to / so that you can / to be able to
To be able to *enter that class, you must first take a test.*

 C Listen again for the phrases that use conditions and mark the statements below true (**T**) or false (**F**).

1 To be able to get into a small class, you must sign up for the advanced lessons. T / F
2 The gold-covered book is used for the beginners' class only. T / F
3 In order to determine your level, an interview is necessary. T / F
4 If you study hard, you can choose the day and time of the class you want. T / F

Talk It Over

Work with a partner. Use the phrases for conditions to discuss your own concerns about English study.

> In order to take an advanced class, we have to know a lot of vocabulary.

> Yes, and we need to study hard so that we can become fluent.

Lesson B *I don't think it's so hard.*

Before You Listen

A Draw lines to match the vocabulary items in blue on the left with their correct meaning on the right.

1	pick up some useful phrases	a	together with its surroundings
2	that never dawned on me	b	learn
3	option	c	many
4	brush up on your grammar	d	occurred to
5	see the word in context	e	choice
6	learn tons of new words	f	review

B Read the statements below and circle a number to show how strongly you agree with each statement. (**1** = disagree strongly, **5** = agree strongly)

1 Teachers should give students options for their classroom learning activities. 1 2 3 4 5
2 In vocabulary tests, students should see the words in some kind of context. 1 2 3 4 5
3 Listening to music helps students to pick up tons of useful phrases. 1 2 3 4 5
4 It's more important to brush up on your grammar than to practice pronunciation. 1 2 3 4 5
5 It never dawned on me that listening to music in English is a useful exercise. 1 2 3 4 5

Extended Listening

A The teacher has given her students a task. Listen to a group of four students talk about various activities for learning English. Number these activities in the order that you hear them.

a Listening to music _____
b Taking vocabulary tests _____
c Videotaping conversations _____
d Watching news _____

B Listen again. How does the group generally feel? Mark the statements below true (**T**) or false (**F**).

1 They all think vocabulary tests are useful. T / F
2 They think listening to music will help improve their English. T / F
3 They think watching news is an easy way to learn English. T / F
4 They think that videotaping their spoken English is a bad idea. T / F

Conversation Strategy: *Giving opinions*

> ▶ When giving their opinions, people often begin with *I think . . .* or *I don't think . . .*
>
> **A:** I don't think that's very useful.
> **B:** I don't think so either.

C Listen again and complete the sentences below with *I think* or *I don't think*.

1 _____ it's great that she's asking us.

2 _____ that memorizing lists of words will help us.

3 _____ music is a good way to study English.

4 _____ it's necessary for us to hear or watch the news.

5 _____ it'll help us to find our grammar and pronunciation mistakes.

Catch It! Listening for negatives

A When agreeing with an opinion, it's necessary to listen carefully for whether it's a negative opinion (contains *not* or *n't*) or a positive opinion (without *not* or *n't*). If it's a negative opinion, speakers use the negative in their response.

A: I don't think it's interesting.
B: I don't think so, either.

B Listen and choose the correct response. Check the appropriate box in the chart.

	1	2	3	4	5	6	7
I think so							
I don't think so, either							

Try It Out!

Prepare a few opinions of your own about good and bad ways to learn English. Discuss them with a partner.

Example:

A: I think we should read English to learn vocabulary. It's better than memorizing vocabulary lists.
B: I think so too. And I don't think song lyrics teach us good vocabulary.
A: I don't think so either.

Education for Life

Lesson A · *Sure, why not?*

Warm-up

 A Complete each sentence with the correct word from the box. You may use a dictionary. Then listen and check.

> retention   subsidize   incentives   certification   expertise   competitive

1 Companies should only employ workers with official _____ from a recognized center of learning.   A / D

2 In a _____ market, companies must allow workers to improve their skills.   A / D

3 Companies should _____ employees who want to take classes in order to do a better job.   A / D

4 Companies should offer strong _____ for workers to continue their education.   A / D

5 It is a worker's responsibility, not the company's, to build the worker's _____.   A / D

6 Companies interested in employee _____ must offer good working conditions.   A / D

B Read the statements in **A** again and decide whether you agree or disagree. Circle **A** or **D**. Discuss with your partner.

Listening

 A Listen to four public relations officers talk about the value of continuing education for their workers. Number the industries they talk about 1–4.

a ☐ car manufacturing

b ☐ electronics

c ☐ law

d ☐ retail sales

B Listen again. Which statement best summarizes the public relations officer's point about their company's program? Number them **1–4** in the order you hear them.

a _____ Workers can choose between attending classes at a university or at the company's on-site study center.

b _____ Spending company money on employee education helps the company keep workers, instead of losing them to other jobs.

c _____ Spending company money on employee education makes workers more productive, which benefits the company financially.

d _____ Workers can choose to pursue another degree or study for professional certification.

Further Listening

A Listen to four conversations about "going back to school." What is the relationship between the speakers? Number the relationships **1–4**.

a brother and sister _____   c old friends   _____
b married couple   _____   d co-workers   _____

B Listen again. What do they plan to **give up**? Circle **a** or **b**.

1 **a** a law career   **b** a career in psychology
2 **a** an office job   **b** a coaching job
3 **a** a sales job   **b** a nursing job
4 **a** a modeling career   **b** a job in finance

Language Focus: *Hedging approval*

▸ Use these phrases to show that you're not 100 percent certain you agree.

I guess it's OK / it should be alright / it probably won't hurt / it couldn't hurt
*If you want to quit your job and travel the world, **I guess it's OK**.*

C Listen again. Decide whether the person speaking is **doubtful** or **certain** in his or her approval, and check the correct box.

	1	2	3	4
doubtful				
certain				

Talk It Over

Create a list of some jobs that interest you and share it with your partner. Be sure to use your new phrases when you talk about them.

> So, I was planning to give up my career as a doctor and work with refugees abroad.

> It should be alright . . . what does your family say about that?

Before You Listen

A   Look at this list of software programs and hardware. Circle the ones you've used before.

- spreadsheet
- contact database
- music organizing software
- photo-editing

- language-learning software
- calendar
- video camera
- microphone and headphones

- presentation software
- spy software
- web browser
- scanner

B   Read the sentences. Do you agree (**A**) or disagree (**D**) with them? Compare your answers with a partner's.

1   Everybody should understand the basics of using a computer.   A / D
2   Computers are necessary tools for learning.   A / D
3   Distance learning via computer is as effective as classroom learning.   A / D
4   Companies should pay for workers to learn how to use computers.   A / D

Extended Listening

 A   A father is asking his daughter for computer advice. Number the kinds of software they mention in the order you hear them, **1–6**.

a _____ video conferencing
b _____ presentation
c _____ e-mail program
d _____ schedule/to-do list
e _____ spreadsheet
f _____ audio surveillance

 B   Listen again. Decide if each of the statements below is true (**T**) or false (**F**).

1   The father must learn how to use a computer because he doesn't want a secretary.   T / F
2   He believes video calls have a stronger impact than audio calls.   T / F
3   He has a high opinion of the work done by the PR department.   T / F
4   He wants to know what the employees at the company say about him.   T / F

Conversation Strategy: *Asking for explanation*

▸ When people don't understand comments or instructions, they often ask for further explanation using the phrase "What do you mean?"

A: You have to double-click the icon with your mouse.
B: What do you mean?

 C Listen and draw a line to connect the word or phrase on the left with the explanation the speaker gives on the right.

1	illegal	**a**	stupid
2	not sharp	**b**	scared into working harder
3	psychologically effective	**c**	against the law

Catch It! Listening for consonants

 A Learners sometimes confuse certain similar-sounding words spoken in standard English. Listen to the statements and circle the best response.

Example: **Statement:** He doesn't want to take a sip.

Response: **a** Maybe he's not thirsty.

b Maybe he'd rather take a plane.

 B Listen to the statements and choose the best response. Circle **a** or **b**.

1 a	I can make it shorter.	**b**	I'll correct it.
2 a	OK. What will you cook?	**b**	Why . . . are you hot?
3 a	I can if you really need it.	**b**	I think we should go left.
4 a	We can make it well.	**b**	We can make it fit.
5 a	The paper or plastic one?	**b**	What's wrong with the front?
6 a	It's getting bigger.	**b**	It's getting brighter.
7 a	Yeah, I got the money.	**b**	Yeah, I got the meaning.

Try It Out!

If you could study something you really enjoy, what would you like to study? Discuss it with a partner. Be sure to use "What do you mean?" if you need more explanation from your partner.

Attitudes Toward Work **3**

Warm-up

 A Complete the e-mail below using the vocabulary in the box. Listen and check your answers.

> dental care   health insurance   parental leave   recession   spokesperson   yacht

Despite the recent economic _____, I got a great position as a _____ for a big, new company. The salary isn't so great, but the benefits include paid vacations, summer parties on the company _____, and extended _____. And the _____ even covers _____. I was thinking, "what's the catch?" but I learned that there are no bad points at all—I'll have a nice office with state-of-the-art equipment to use.

B What are the most important points about a job, in your opinion? Make a list of five things and share your answers with a partner.

Listening

 A Listen to the news stories about employment changes in four countries. Number the news topics in the order you hear them.

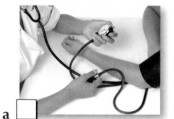
a ☐ universal health care

b ☐ decline of labor unions

c ☐ parental leave

d ☐ recession

 B Listen again and decide whether the statements below are true (**T**) or false (**F**).

1 The new Swedish law applies to both women and men. T / F
2 The financial news from the USA is positive for most companies. T / F
3 The New Zealand government plans to pay 100 percent of worker health care. T / F
4 Workers' salaries in Japan have risen along with corporate profits. T / F

Further Listening

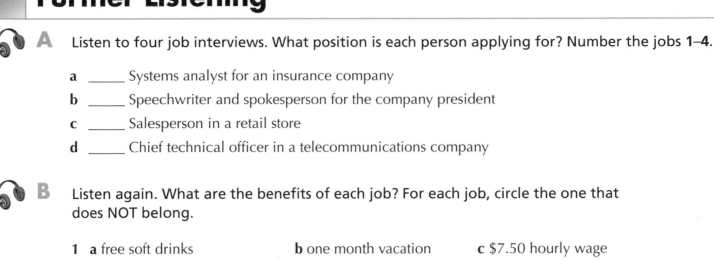

A Listen to four job interviews. What position is each person applying for? Number the jobs **1–4**.

a _____ Systems analyst for an insurance company

b _____ Speechwriter and spokesperson for the company president

c _____ Salesperson in a retail store

d _____ Chief technical officer in a telecommunications company

B Listen again. What are the benefits of each job? For each job, circle the one that does NOT belong.

1 **a** free soft drinks	**b** one month vacation	**c** $7.50 hourly wage
2 **a** dental insurance	**b** regular salary raises	**c** use of company vacation resorts
3 **a** comfortable travel	**b** one personal assistant	**c** excellent equipment
4 **a** free donuts every morning	**b** a computer	**c** a company calendar

Language Focus: *Softening in formal situations*

▸ Use these phrases to introduce a point that the listener might not like:

I just want to let you know / inform you / make you aware / alert you . . .
Please be advised / informed that . . .
I just want to inform you *that we don't carry health insurance.*

C Listen again for the phrases that soften the job's negative points. Match the point to the job.

1 _____   2 _____   3 _____   4 _____

a There's no pay for overtime work.

b Working conditions are very strict.

c The boss is a difficult person to work for.

d Health insurance isn't covered for the first three months of employment.

Talk It Over

Imagine you are interviewing applicants for a job at your company. Work with a partner and tell him or her three benefits of the job. Use your new phrases to soften the negative points. Take turns role-playing with different partners.

> I want to make you aware that we offer only five vacation days a year.

> Oh really? Well, I'll have to think about it.

Lesson B   *It sounds like a good deal.*

Before You Listen

 A   Draw lines to match the vocabulary items in blue on the left with their definitions on the right. Listen and check.

1 benefits   **a** workers leaving, new workers beginning

2 high turnover   **b** stop working until the company gives workers something they have asked for

3 go on strike   **c** the total number of employees of a company

4 workforce   **d** good things you get from your job, in addition to pay

5 layoffs   **e** workers fired because there is no more work for them

B   Read the sentences. Do you agree (**A**) or disagree (**D**) with them? Circle the letter and compare your answers with those of a partner.

1 It's good for the workforce to form labor unions and go on strike.   A / D

2 High turnover affects a company's profits.   A / D

3 Research and Development is the most important part of a company.   A / D

4 Men and women should have equal pay and benefits.   A / D

Extended Listening

 A   At the International Conference of Skilled Workers, four people are talking about working conditions in their countries. Next to each worker's name, write the name of the country they come from and circle their job.

Yung Jun _____   **Rose** _____   **Vikram** _____   **Astrid** _____

a financial researcher   **a** metal worker   **a** farm equipment producer   **a** engineer

b drug manufacturer   **b** auto worker   **b** farmer   **b** nurse

 B   Listen again. Fill in the table as they give details about their jobs.

Name	Job security	Paid parental leave	Vacations
Rose	10 yrs ago: bad; now: workers are more _____	_____ months	Up to _____ days
Yung Jun	_____% have good job security; union membership only _____%	3 months	_____ days
Vikram	Difficult to fire people; government watches companies carefully	_____ months	1 day off for every _____ days worked
Astrid	Workers have open _____; union membership is high	_____ months	25–32 days

Conversation Strategy: *Making a summary comment*

▸ To show a speaker that you understand a point they have made, you can make a summary comment beginning with the words, "It sounds like . . ."

A: Our managers allow us to make decisions for ourselves.
B: It sounds like you have a lot of freedom in your job.

 C Connect the summary comment with the country or countries the speaker is talking about.

1 It sounds like you guys are really ready to compete internationally.   India

2 It sounds like workers there are tough.   Sweden

3 It sounds like unions there are really organized.   Brazil

South Korea

Catch It! Contrastive stress

 A English speakers often emphasize certain words by placing a heavy stress on the word.

Example: He's not *ready*.
He's not ready.

Listen carefully for the word that is stressed. Choose the correct response. For example:

Statement: *He's* not ready.
Response: **a** Who isn't?   **b** Why not?

 B Listen to the statements and circle the appropriate response.

1 **a** Who is?	**b** Why?	5 **a** She will?	**b** How long?
2 **a** Who does?	**b** Sign what?	6 **a** Who does?	**b** How?
3 **a** She feels what?	**b** About what?	7 **a** Who are?	**b** How?
4 **a** What is?	**b** Is it?		

Try It Out!

Work with a partner and talk about a job you had or the job you have now. Make sure you use "It sounds like . . ." to comment on your partner's points.

Hobbies

Lesson A   *I'd love to, but . . .*

Warm-up

A Look at the list of hobbies below. What's your opinion about each one? Write the letters (**F**) for fun, (**D**) for difficult, and (**E**) for expensive. Then share your opinions with a partner.

1 _____ cooking   4 _____ playing chess   7 _____ drawing

2 _____ bowling   5 _____ cycling   8 _____ hiking

3 _____ camping   6 _____ dancing   9 _____ gardening

B Read the sentences. Do you agree (**A**) or disagree (**D**) with them? Use a dictionary for any words you don't understand. Circle your answer and compare your opinions with those of a partner.

1 Everyone should have at least one hobby, for example, juggling or drawing.   A / D

2 It's easy to become obsessed with a hobby like photography.   A / D

3 The main purpose of a hobby like scuba-diving is recreation.   A / D

4 I prefer hobbies that I can do alone, such as knitting or writing to pen pals. A / D

Listening

  A Listen to four people talk about their past and present hobbies. Which hobby does each speaker still do now? Circle **a** or **b**.

1

a   b

2

a   b

3

a   b

4

a   b

  B Listen again. What is their complaint about their present hobby? Circle the correct answer.

1 **a** too expensive   **b** dislike traveling   **c** equipment is heavy

2 **a** takes a lot of time **b** dislike the Internet   **c** digging is painful

3 **a** too expensive   **b** dislike weight gain   **c** too much work

4 **a** too old-fashioned   **b** dislike doing it at home **c** heavy to carry

Further Listening

A Listen to four conversations. Number the hobbies (**1–4**) in the order you hear them.

B Listen again. Fill in the missing words to summarize their talks.

1 He learned _____ from his father and hunts deer with his _____.

2 He makes _____ of people's _____.

3 You can juggle _____ once you learn the basic _____.

4 She formed a _____ for the women's bowling _____.

Language Focus: *Refusing politely*

▸ Use these phrases to politely refuse invitations.

I'd really love to, but . . . / I'm afraid . . . / I have a problem with . . .
I'd really love to, but *I've already made other plans.*

C Listen again for the phrases that begin the refusal and decide if each statement is true (**T**) or false (**F**).

1 She is too busy after Christmas to hunt.   T / F
2 He worries that he is more talented than the artist.   T / F
3 He isn't interested in learning her hobby.   T / F
4 She would rather have a romantic Saturday night.   T / F

Talk It Over

Tell your partner about your favorite hobby and invite him or her to participate in it with you. Be sure to use the phrases for refusing politely when your partner invites you to share in his or her hobby.

Why don't you come over to help me do some gardening?

I'd really love to, but I don't think I'd be very good at that.

Before You Listen

 A   Match the words and phrases you will hear in this lesson with their definitions. Listen and check.

1	nuclear weapon	**a**	instructions on how to cook something
2	recipe	**b**	the city or town where the government of a country or state meets
3	saddle	**c**	a powerful bomb that explodes using atomic energy
4	capital	**d**	a leather seat you put on the back of a horse to ride it

B   In the **Extended Listening** below, the president of a country is talking about his hobbies. What do you think the leader of your country does in his or her free time? Discuss with a partner.

Extended Listening

 A   Listen to the press conference. The president is talking about the hobbies that he enjoys doing during his vacation. Circle the activities that he says he's been doing lately.

1	reading books	**6**	horseback riding
2	playing cards	**7**	studying geography
3	cooking	**8**	dancing
4	traveling	**9**	reading comics
5	hunting	**10**	watching TV

 B   Sometimes we can receive information and understand things from what is NOT actually said; in other words, we infer it. Listen again and circle yes (**Y**) for what is inferred here and no (**N**) for what is not inferred.

1	The press secretary helps the president to express himself more clearly.	Y / N
2	The president has a large family.	Y / N
3	The president does not like cooking.	Y / N
4	The reporters think the president doesn't spend enough time working.	Y / N
5	The reporters are surprised that the president is studying state capitals.	Y / N

▶ To show listeners that they're searching for a specific word or phrase, people often use phrases like these:

What's the word? / What do you call it?

 C Listen again and number the words or phrases that the president searches for in the order you hear them. Three are not used.

a _____ saddle **e** _____ foreign relations

b _____ economy **f** _____ state capitols

c _____ comics **g** _____ recipe

d _____ nuclear weapons **h** _____ environment

Catch It! Homophones

A Some English words have different meanings but identical pronunciations.

write / right

 B Listen to each sentence and circle the word the speaker uses.

1 its it's **5** flower flour

2 site sight **6** weather whether

3 their they're **7** weight wait

4 whole hole

Try It Out!

Tell your partner about some hobbies that you haven't tried yet but would like to. When you can't think of a word, be sure to use your new phrases to show your partner you're searching for the right word.

Reading

Lesson A   *Be certain to come prepared!*

Warm-up

A   Look at the book genres below. Use a dictionary for the ones you don't know, then decide if they are fiction (**F**) or nonfiction (**NF**). The first one has been done for you. Listen and check.

1 __F__ science fiction
2 _____ biography
3 _____ essay
4 _____ fantasy
5 _____ history
6 _____ mystery

7 _____ short stories
8 _____ politics/current affairs
9 _____ romance
10 _____ self-improvement
11 _____ thriller
12 _____ philosophy

B   Put a check mark (✔) next to the genres that you have read before. Circle the genres that you enjoy the most. Discuss with a partner.

Listening

A   Listen to four people talk about what they read. Who is the author of the last book that each person read?

1 **a** Tom Clancy   **b** Robert Ludlum

2 **a** Danielle Steele   **b** Dale Carnegie

3 **a** Greg Palast   **b** Agatha Christie

4 **a** J. R. R. Tolkien **b** Ursula K. LeGuin

B   Listen again and decide if the statements below are true (**T**) or false (**F**). Circle the correct answer.

1   The speaker generally doesn't read fiction.   T / F
2   *Self-improvement* books are great "escape reading."   T / F
3   The speaker was surprised that the book wasn't more difficult to understand. T / F
4   The speaker is now more interested in politics than reading fantasy books.   T / F

Further Listening

 A Some people have joined a book discussion group at a community library. What rules does the librarian explain to the group? Number them in the order you hear them. One is not used.

a All members must speak in the group discussion. _____

b People must give presentations summarizing their opinions. _____

c There are special rules about eating and drinking during meetings. _____

d People must read the entire book before the meeting. _____

e As long as you own the book, read with a pencil in your hand. _____

B Listen again. What other information is explained? Fill in the blanks to summarize the main message in each dialogue. Note: Some of these sentences are not phrased exactly as you hear them.

1 If the book has been _____ from the library, you mustn't put a _____ in it.

2 If, more than once, you are not _____, you'll be asked not to _____ further meetings.

3 _____ participation is mandatory; _____ silently will not be tolerated.

4 Coffee is _____ in the meeting room, but be careful not to _____ any.

Language Focus: *Pointing out information*

▶ You can use these phrases to introduce important rules or points:

Please be sure / be informed / be advised / don't forget / be certain
Please be certain not to leave anything behind when you go.

 C Listen again for the phrases and match them to complete the sentences.

1 Please be sure   **a** that there are a few basic rules.

2 Be informed   **b** that the book belongs to you.

3 Don't forget   **c** that all members are expected to give their opinions.

4 Be advised   **d** that those who are ill-prepared will receive a warning.

Talk It Over

Role-play with your partner. Pretend to lend him or her something of yours and use the phrases above.

> Here's my electronic dictionary. Please be sure that you don't drop it and break it!

> Thanks, and here's my English novel. Don't forget to return it next week!

Before You Listen

 A   Match the words and phrases you will hear in this lesson with their definitions. Listen and check.

1	alien	**a**	a standard or typical version of something
2	demon	**b**	having a powerful effect on people
3	stereotype	**c**	event or action that affects society
4	pseudo-	**d**	the belief that the position of the stars can affect people's lives
5	astrology	**e**	not real, fake
6	influential	**f**	(in this context) a being from another planet
7	social change	**g**	a spirit believed to be evil

B   Some people believe strongly in things like demons, astrology, and aliens. What about you? Discuss your opinions with a partner.

Extended Listening

 A   In the break room at their school, four teachers are talking about some of the books they've read. What phrase best summarizes the speaker's point about the book he or she is recommending. Circle **a**, **b**, or **c**.

1 Carl Sagan's *The Demon-Haunted World*
   a scientists are mad
   b the scientific method is important
   c pseudo-science is valuable

2 Ayn Rand's *Atlas Shrugged*
   a people are selfish
   b society needs more barriers
   c individuals shouldn't be prevented
      from doing things

3 Adam Smith's *The Wealth of Nations*
   a capitalism benefits people
   b only money motivates people
   c the market is invisible

4 Howard Zinn's *A People's History of the United States*
   a progress comes from leaders
   b social change is dangerous
   c average people make change

B Listen again and decide whether the statements below are true (**T**) or false (**F**) according to the speakers.

1 When people believe in aliens and fortune-telling, society becomes smarter.   T / F

2 It's selfish for people to live whatever way they want without caring for society in general.   T / F

3 The "invisible hand" of the market fixes the economy automatically.   T / F

4 When people make money by buying and selling, society becomes happier.   T / F

Conversation Strategy: *Guessing the word*

▸ In conversation, sometimes people guess the word or phrase they think the speaker will say next. This is usually a way of showing that they are listening carefully and very interested in what the speaker is saying.

A: It was a great book. I just couldn't . . .
B: . . . put it down.

 C Listen to how other people guess the speaker's next word or phrase. Write the missing word or words in the blanks below.

1 . . . the problem of pseudo-science, for example, astrology and fortune-telling, believing in angels or witches, or . . . _____

2 . . . and if society puts up any, um, . . . _____

3 . . . from the owner of a company, down to . . . _____

4 . . . women who fought for their right to vote, you know, more than just car— _____

Catch It! Voiced and voiceless consonants

A Put your hand on your throat. If your voice box moves when you say the consonant, the consonant is voiced. If it doesn't move, the consonant is voiceless.

Examples: "cheap"   The /ch/ sound is voiceless.
               "sheep"   The /sh/ sound is voiceless.
               "jeep"   The /j/ sound is voiced.

B Listen to the first sounds of the words. Decide whether each is voiced or voiceless and check the correct box.

	1	2	3	4	5	6	7
Voiced							
Voiceless							

Try It Out!

Work with a partner and talk about one of your favorite books. The person listening should try to guess a word or phrase that the person speaking will say next.

Example:
A: I read *Anne of Green Gables*. It's about a couple who adopt a boy but, instead of a boy, they get . . .
B: A girl.

Consumerism

6

Buying is believing!

Warm-up

A   Look at the list of words and phrases below. Which are from the world of business (**B**), and which are used to discuss the environment (**E**)? Write **B** or **E**. Some may be both.

1 _____ cutting-edge technology
2 __E__ ecosystem
3 _____ greenhouse gases
4 _____ market share
5 _____ marketing campaign
6 _____ planting trees
7 _____ solar panels

8 _____ public relations
9 _____ recycling paper
10 _____ reduce emissions
11 _____ renewable energy
12 _____ research
13 _____ the ozone layer
14 _____ wind turbine generators

B   Compare your answers with those of a partner. What does each of the words or phrases mean? Explain to your partner.

Listening

   A   Listen to four television commercials promoting different companies. What is each company's principal business? Circle **a** or **b**.

1   **a** oil production   **b** products to clean the environment
2   **a** chemical production   **b** beauty products
3   **a** energy production   **b** travel agency
4   **a** trash management   **b** paper production

   B   Listen again and decide what the public relations purpose of each commercial is. Circle **a** or **b**.

1   **a** efforts for a cleaner environment
    b promise to use less oil
2   **a** image as beautiful and perfect
    b products as all-natural and animal-friendly
3   **a** progress throughout human history
    b development of energy sources other than coal, oil, and gas.
4   **a** campaign to recycle paper and plant trees
    b commitment to renewable energy

Further Listening

A Listen to a company president talking to four executive employees. Match each employee to his or her position in the company.

1 Michael   **a** Research & Development
2 Kaori   **b** Manufacturing & Production
3 Zach   **a** International Sales
4 Shuang   **b** Image & Advertising

B Listen again. Fill in the missing information about the company's new product, the Quasar PDA (Personal Digital Assistant).

1 The Mega-Quasar's price is US$ _____ and the product has _____ percent of the world market for PDAs.

2 The next generation of the product will have a _____ function with _____-recognition.

3 The company president wants to use Cameron Diaz's face to promote the product in _____.

4 The factory produces _____ units per week, resulting in _____ million Quasars a year.

Language Focus: *Interrupting politely*

▸ You can use these phrases to show politeness, especially if you feel you're interrupting someone who is busy with their work or something else.

Sorry to interrupt you / I hope I'm not bothering you / Do you have a moment? / Can I have just a second of your time?

A: Excuse me, do you have a moment? I'd like to tell you about the new report.
B: Sure, go ahead.

C Listen again for the phrases that begin the interruption. Number them in the order you hear them.

a Excuse me, sorry to interrupt you. _____
b I hope I'm not bothering you. _____
c Do you have a moment? _____
d Can I have just a second of your time? _____

Talk It Over

Role-play with your partner: One of you is the boss, the other is an employee. Report some important information to the boss.

> Excuse me, do you have a moment? I'd like to tell you about our problem in sales.

> OK, what's the problem?

Before You Listen

A Match the expression on the left with the idea it represents.

Expression

1 Shop 'til you drop
2 You have to help the economy
3 Conspicuous consumption
4 Money to throw away
5 Buy now, pay later
6 Pre-empt an urge
7 Open a can of worms

Represents the idea that . . .

a Introduce a topic that will be difficult to explain
b Prevent the feeling that you must do something
c Go on a shopping spree—buy a lot of things
d Shopping supports society
e Showing off expensive items in order to impress people
f You can spend money easily because you are very rich
g Using credit cards allows you to spend money you don't have

B What is your opinion about shopping? Do you think people should buy whatever they want or should they only buy what they need? Discuss with a partner.

Extended Listening

A Sung Li is preparing her class presentation on the causes and effects of consumerism. Listen to the discussion with her teacher and put the presentation slides in order.

a Consumption's effect on the environment   _____
b How to consume less   _____
c People's need to consume   _____
d Consumption's effect on personal finances   _____
e Consumption as the solution to dissatisfaction   _____
f The theory of "conspicuous consumption"   _____

B Listen again. Read the statements below. Would the student giving the presentation agree (**A**) or disagree (**D**)? Circle **A** or **D**.

1 Humans have an internal need to buy things.   A / D

2 Governments hope that if people are busy shopping, they won't care about more important issues.   A / D

3 The theory of conspicuous consumption says that people who show their wealth gain status and respect.   A / D

4 Living in a consumer culture is stressful.   A / D

5 Shopping makes people feel satisfied.   A / D

6 It is almost impossible to get people to buy less in a consumer culture.   A / D

▸ We often use phrases like these to show that we're thinking about how to give a bigger explanation.

It's difficult to explain . . . / How can I say it?

 C The student uses the phrases above three times as she struggles to explain her points. Number the points (**1–3**) in the order you hear them.

a When people see a person with expensive things, the person is automatically given respect. _____

b People can act to stop unnecessary consumption. _____

c The belief that "shopping is entertainment" is a trick of the media. _____

Catch It! Missing sounds

 A In the pronunciation of some words in English, sounds are sometimes dropped.

Example: "Fifth" is sometimes pronounced without the second /f/, so it sounds like /fith/. Listen to the example.

B Listen to the sentences and circle the letters that are not pronounced.

1 I'm going away in February.
2 I don't often go to the movies.
3 Did you give the letter to the postman?
4 You can't dance to folk music.
5 I think she was taking a bath.
6 I asked him a question.
7 Did you get many gifts for your birthday?

Try It Out!

In your opinion, what are the positive and negative effects of consumerism? Make a list. Work with a partner and discuss consumerism.

Positive	Negative

Part 1

For each question, you will see a photograph and hear four short sentences. You will not see the sentences in writing, so you must listen carefully. The sentences will be spoken one time only. Choose the sentence that best describes what you see in the photo. Each question is two points.

1 a b c d

2 a b c d

3 a b c d

4   a   b   c   d

5   a   b   c   d

6   a   b   c   d

Part 2

For each question, you will hear a question or statement and three responses. You will not see the question or responses in writing, so you must listen carefully. They will be spoken one time only. Choose the best response to the question or statement.

7   a   b   c

8   a   b   c

9   a   b   c

10   a   b   c

11   a   b   c

12   a   b   c

13   a   b   c

Part 3

You will hear two conversations. Listen to each conversation, and choose the best response to each question. You will not see the conversations in writing, so you must listen carefully. You will hear each conversation one time only.

Conversation 1

14 What is their relationship?

    a friends

    b colleagues

    c a couple

    d an instructor and a learner

15 Where are they now?

    a in a cafeteria   **b** in the woman's office

    c in the man's office   **d** in a post office

16 What is the man probably going to do with her report?

    a get rid of it   **b** find out the due date

    c check it later   **d** put it in the box

Conversation 2

17 What is the woman's first language?

    a Korean   **b** Japanese

    c English   **d** Spanish

18 What does the man say about his own language ability?

    a He only speaks one language.

    b He confuses his Spanish and Italian vocabulary.

    c He can't distinguish between Japanese and Korean sounds.

    d He can't learn Korean.

19 What are they probably going to do next?

    a The woman will teach the man some Korean phrases.

    b The woman will teach the man some Japanese phrases.

    c The man will go to Korea with the woman.

    d The man and the woman will compare two languages.

Part 4

You will hear two short talks. Listen to each talk, and choose the best response to each question. You will not see the talks in writing, so you must listen carefully. You will hear each talk one time only.

Talk 1

20 What is the book about?
   a how television has affected people's thinking ability
   b how consumer culture has made people unreasonable
   c the environmental effects of consumerism
   d television's damage to the environment

21 What was different about people 150 years ago?
   a They used to be unable to listen to public debates.
   b They used to think in terms of a printed text.
   c They learned from political speeches.
   d They were more patient and sociable than people now.

22 Why does the speaker say television is responsible for the change?
   a The quality of television programming has declined.
   b It has made the public less interested in politics.
   c It makes people get ideas from images, not from written words.
   d Political programs on TV are too complex.

Talk 2

23 What did his father do?
   a He became a teacher later in his life.
   b He became a student later in his life.
   c He became a government researcher.
   d He moved to Zimbabwe.

24 According to the speaker, what is wrong with memorizing facts?
   a It's not the best way for children to learn.
   b Children's minds aren't open enough.
   c Children's minds are too flexible.
   d It takes too much time.

25 According to the speaker, what should be the main purpose of education?
   a to teach adults to understand the world
   b to teach people how to ask good questions
   c to teach people about problems in foreign countries
   d to encourage people to study as they get older

Practice Test 1 Answer Sheet

Part 1

1 (a) (b) (c) (d)   4 (a) (b) (c) (d)
2 (a) (b) (c) (d)   5 (a) (b) (c) (d)
3 (a) (b) (c) (d)   6 (a) (b) (c) (d)

Part 2

7   (a) (b) (c)   11 (a) (b) (c)
8   (a) (b) (c)   12 (a) (b) (c)
9   (a) (b) (c)   13 (a) (b) (c)
10 (a) (b) (c)

Part 3

14 (a) (b) (c) (d)   17 (a) (b) (c) (d)
15 (a) (b) (c) (d)   18 (a) (b) (c) (d)
16 (a) (b) (c) (d)   19 (a) (b) (c) (d)

Part 4

20 (a) (b) (c) (d)   23 (a) (b) (c) (d)
21 (a) (b) (c) (d)   24 (a) (b) (c) (d)
22 (a) (b) (c) (d)   25 (a) (b) (c) (d)

Ideal Partner

Lesson A — *Fortunately, they both have great jobs!*

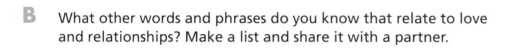

Warm-up

A   Match the words and phrases you will hear in this lesson to their definitions. Listen and check.

1	sense of belonging	**a**	explain something so it becomes clear
2	immature	**b**	a special holiday for a couple after they get married
3	honeymoon	**c**	secure about money
4	shed some light on	**d**	a person who has promised to marry
5	all sunshine	**e**	fix problems
6	work out issues	**f**	informal way of saying "to get married"
7	tie the knot	**g**	a promise to be married
8	on firm financial ground	**h**	behaving like a young child
9	engagement	**i**	always happy
10	fiancé(e)	**j**	feeling of being part of a group

B   What other words and phrases do you know that relate to love and relationships? Make a list and share it with a partner.

Listening

A   Listen to four people talk about their last partner. What do they say is the most important point for compatibility? Circle **a** or **b**.

1	**a** a strong physical attraction	**b** a strong emotional connection
2	**a** a man who is mature	**b** a man who wants children
3	**a** a similar cultural background	**b** a strong spiritual connection
4	**a** similar interests	**b** similar political beliefs

B   Listen again. Is the speaker generally optimistic or pessimistic about finding a good partner? Circle the correct answer.

1	**a** optimistic	**b** pessimistic	**3**	**a** optimistic	**b** pessimistic
2	**a** optimistic	**b** pessimistic	**4**	**a** optimistic	**b** pessimistic

Further Listening

 A Listen to four conversations at a wedding reception. What is each speaker's relationship to the married couple? Circle **a** or **b**.

1 **a** new friend of the groom   **b** old friend of the groom
2 **a** friend of the groom   **b** friend of the bride
3 **a** co-worker of the bride   **b** high school friend of the bride
4 **a** baby-sitters   **b** mothers of the bride and groom

B Remember that we can receive information and understand things from what is NOT actually said, in other words, what is *inferred*. Listen again and circle yes (**Y**) for what is inferred here and no (**N**) for what is not inferred.

❶ **a** She used to complain to him about his cell phone.   Y / N
   b He didn't look through her purse when they were dating.   Y / N
❷ The couple gets along well because they are so similar.   Y / N
❸ **a** She seems to her co-workers to be very professional.   Y / N
   b The couple knew each other for a long time before they married.   Y / N
   c The groom hopes to become a doctor.   Y / N
❹ The couple plans to start a family very soon.   Y / N

Language Focus: *Emphasizing an attitude*

▸ We sometimes use adverbs at the beginning of a sentence to emphasize our attitude about what we are saying.

Fortunately / Obviously / Ideally / Hopefully
I hope it won't rain on the wedding party: **Hopefully**, *it won't rain on the wedding party.*
I think it's good that they get along well: **Fortunately**, *they get along well.*

 C Listen again for the adverbs (**a–d**) and match them to the paraphrased ideas (**1–4**).

1 They wish for the couple to have no problems trusting each other.   **a** fortunately
2 It's clear that they get along better than we guessed.   **b** obviously
3 It's a good thing they have jobs with good salaries.   **c** ideally
4 It would be great if they had children soon.   **d** hopefully

Talk It Over

Create a list of a few qualities that you look for in a romantic partner and a few qualities you hope to avoid. Be sure to use your new words for emphasizing when you talk with a partner.

> I think intelligence is very important. Hopefully, my partner will have a good education.

> I know what you mean. Ideally, a smart person is the best!

Before You Listen

 A   Match the words or phrases you will hear in this lesson to their definitions. Listen and check.

1	to have issues	**a**	to act passively
2	to vent feelings	**b**	creating a home
3	to forgo something	**c**	to have problems
4	to give someone some space	**d**	to complain openly
5	to be proactive	**e**	to not be able to get along together
6	to go with the flow	**f**	to go without or to give up something
7	to be incompatible	**g**	to manage a situation calmly
8	to deal with conflict	**h**	to avoid a problem by taking positive action
9	nest-building	**i**	to face and resolve problems
10	to take something in one's stride	**j**	to let someone have quiet time alone

B   Discuss with a partner. Is there anything in your life recently that you could describe using one or more of the phrases above?

Extended Listening

 A   A married couple visits a marriage counselor for advice. Mark the topics they discuss in the order you hear them. One is not used.

a Their fights about their jobs   _____
b How they deal with conflict   _____
c How compatible they are together _____
d The goals they share as a couple   _____

 B   Listen again. Decide if each statement below is true (**T**) or false (**F**).

1	Despite their differences, their personalities generally fit well together.	T / F
2	He is not too bothered by her quick temper because she quickly cools down.	T / F
3	She feels attacked when he is venting his emotions.	T / F
4	The counselor is pessimistic about her ability to help them.	T / F

▶ To show someone that you understand what they have said, you can begin your restatement of their main point with one of these phrases:

So, you mean . . . / So, you're saying . . .
A: I'm really not hungry.
B: So, you're saying you don't want to have lunch?

C Listen again. Complete the sentences below.

1 _____ having a house and raising a family, or nest-building, is less important to you than your personal growth.

2 _____ he sees when you're flooding with emotion and he gives you some space.

3 _____ you have issues about fighting, especially about money and how much time you spend together.

Catch It! Reconstructing ellipses

A English speakers often shorten their sentences when they speak. For example, a speaker might say, "Ya tired?" and we understand that they mean "Are you tired?"

B Listen to these shortened sentences and fill in the blank with the full form to complete the meaning.

1 _____ yet?
2 _____ a date this weekend?
3 _____ with me.
4 _____ rain tonight.
5 _____ get along well?
6 _____ the man of your dreams?
7 _____ swimming together?

Try It Out!

Work with a partner and talk about what's important to you in a relationship. Make sure you both use your new phrases (*So, you mean . . . / So, you're saying . . .*) to show that you've understood what the other person has said.

Example:
A: A good sense of humor is important to me.
B: So, you're saying you want someone who makes you laugh?

Co-workers

8

Lesson A   *There's no reason to quit.*

Warm-up

 A   Match the phrases you will hear in this lesson to their definitions. Listen and check.

1	to create ill-will	**a**	to defend someone or something
2	to keep your distance	**b**	to say unpleasant things
3	to stay on good terms	**c**	to stay away
4	to stand up for	**d**	to cause bad feelings
5	to take a hint	**e**	to keep a good relationship
6	to make snide remarks	**f**	to understand indirectly

B   Read the sentences below. Do you agree (**A**) or disagree (**D**)? Circle your answer.

1 I usually keep my distance from people who make snide remarks.   A / D
2 I admire people who stand up for their beliefs.   A / D
3 I like to stay on good terms with everyone in my family.   A / D

Listening

 A   Listen to four management experts describe four different worker styles. Which point best describes each kind of employee? Circle **a** or **b**.

1 **a** good communicator   **b** good project manager
2 **a** good leader   **b** good at closing a sale
3 **a** gets along with others   **b** satisfied with job
4 **a** imaginative   **b** efficient

 B   Listen again. What's the negative point for each employee type? Circle **a** or **b**.

1 **Expressive:**   **a** often misses work   **b** sometimes rejects others' ideas
2 **Driver:**   **a** resents other workers   **b** gets better job offers
3 **Amiable:**   **a** no special talents   **b** sometimes causes trouble
4 **Creative:**   **a** often unmotivated   **b** not good at following leaders

Further Listening

A Four workers visit the Director of Human Resources at their company to get help with their work-related problem. Number the images that represent each problem.

B Listen again. What does the director tell each person? Complete the sentences.

1 This is an issue that you shouldn't try to fix yourself. . . . I think I can _____.

2 Tell him you're _____ in him romantically.

3 Just _____ me.

4 If you're being bullied, you've come _____.

Language Focus: *Dissuading*

▸ When we want to dissuade a person (persuade him or her not to do something), we sometimes use these phrases at the beginning of a sentence.

There's no need to / reason to / call for . . .

There's no need to *argue with your co-worker about that.*

C Listen again and match the opening phrases with the words that complete the sentence. One is used twice.

1 There's no need to   **a** look for another job

2 There's no call for   **b** direct confrontation

3 There's no reason to   **c** file a company report

                        d quit over this

Talk It Over

Role-play with a partner: One of you is a counselor and the other is a worker or a student with a problem.

> I'm very unhappy because someone in my class has been creating ill-will.

> There's no need to be upset. I'm sure we can deal with this.

Lesson B   *Let's hear some ideas.*

Before You Listen

A   Read the statements below and decide what you think about them. Circle your opinion
from **5** (strongly agree) to **1** (strongly disagree).

1	Team work is more effective than individual work.	5 4 3 2 1
2	People who are good with small details are more valuable than people who have a wider view.	5 4 3 2 1
3	Good communicators are usually excellent leaders.	5 4 3 2 1
4	Creative workers should be paid extra if they have a great idea that makes a lot of money for their company.	5 4 3 2 1
5	Salespeople may be dishonest in order to close a sale.	5 4 3 2 1
6	A worker's salary should be based on performance, not age.	5 4 3 2 1

B   Compare your answers with those of a partner.
Discuss why you chose the answers you did.

Extended Listening

A   In a company meeting, executives are talking about what
type of workers they need for a new product development
team. Listen and fill in the blanks in the meeting notes.

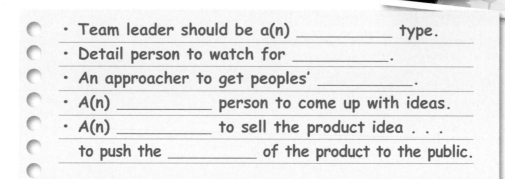

> • Team leader should be a(n) _____ type.
> • Detail person to watch for _____.
> • An approacher to get peoples' _____.
> • A(n) _____ person to come up with ideas.
> • A(n) _____ to sell the product idea . . .
>   to push the _____ of the product to the public.

B   Listen again. Decide whether the group would agree (**A**) or disagree (**D**) with the
following points.

1	The team leader must keep everyone together, but not be too bossy.	A / D
2	A driver type has to have a good eye for detail.	A / D
3	An approacher can make surveys and approach people to get their opinions.	A / D
4	Even a lazy idea person is a valuable member of the team.	A / D
5	A closer must be good with other team members and be good with details.	A / D
6	A closer should be good at communicating with other departments during product development.	A / D

▸ We use certain words in English to show others that we agree with their comments and encourage their ideas.

definitely / absolutely / exactly / brilliant / excellent / perfect

A: I was thinking we could go to a movie since it's raining.
B: *Perfect! Brilliant!*

 C Listen again for the reactions. Number them in the order you hear them.

a Absolutely _____   **d** Excellent _____

b Definitely _____   **e** Brilliant _____

c Perfect _____   **f** Exactly _____

Catch It! *Wh-* and *how* questions

A Sometimes the first word of a *wh-* or *how* question is spoken quickly and can be hard to catch. Look at the question and the two possible replies below. Choose the most accurate reply to show that you heard the question correctly. For example:

Question: How are you going to do it?
Answer: **a** I'll use a hammer.   **b** Because it's broken.

 B Listen carefully to the first word of each question and circle the correct response below.

1 **a** To the library.   **b** Pretty good.
2 **a** By 5 o'clock.   **b** By train.
3 **a** Anything is fine.   **b** Anywhere is fine.
4 **a** In a few hours.   **b** My best friend.
5 **a** At the station.   **b** Around noon.
6 **a** Everybody, probably.   **b** A lot of food, I hope.
7 **a** To San Francisco.   **b** To look for a job.

Try It Out!

Work with a partner and talk about the type of worker you are. If you've never worked in an office, talk about the kind of worker you think you might be. Remember to use words of encouragement.

Example:
A: I think I'm probably a creative type.
B: Absolutely! I am too.

Lesson A   *He was a real genius!*

Warm-up

A People become famous for different reasons. Match the seven types of famous people in the box with the words below. Each word may match more than one category of fame.

> **a** inventors   **b** explorers   **c** artists   **d** philosophers   **e** writers   **f** warriors   **g** leaders

1 _____ wisdom	5 _____ genius	9 _____ battle	13 _____ scholar
2 _____ swordsman	6 _____ poet	10 _____ theorems	14 _____ wealth
3 _____ nobility	7 _____ medicine	11 _____ ethics	15 _____ talent
4 _____ sculptor	8 _____ math	12 _____ bravery	16 _____ risk

B Which category of famous people do you most admire? Why? Tell a partner.

Listening

 A Listen to four speakers talk about an impressive figure in world history. Circle the word that is NOT used to describe each person.

1 **a** artist   **b** genius   **c** philosopher
2 **a** strong   **b** brave   **c** crazy
3 **a** famous   **b** wealthy   **c** philosopher
4 **a** famous   **b** genius   **c** educated

 B Listen again and decide which of the statements below best summarizes the speaker's feelings about the historical person. Circle **a** or **b**.

1 **a** Leonardo da Vinci had many talents and was a man "ahead of his time."
   b His most amazing contribution to history was his invention of the helicopter.
2 **a** Joan of Arc is especially important now that we know that she wasn't mentally ill.
   b Her bravery in battle made her famous at a very young age.
3 **a** Confucius was not only a philosopher, but also a government worker.
   b His ideas about how people should behave toward each other were very influential.
4 **a** Einstein was a natural genius, not a trained scientist.
   b He was a professor.

Further Listening

A Listen to four students talk with their teachers about their history presentations. Whom do they plan to talk about? Circle **a** or **b**.

1 **a** Shakespeare   **b** Chaucer
2 **a** Eleanor Roosevelt   **b** Harriet Tubman
3 **a** Musashi   **b** King Sejong
4 **a** Bach   **b** Mozart

B Listen again. Why did each student choose to speak about that person? Circle **a** or **b**.

1 **a** He wrote the greatest plays in the English language.
   b He took English from a common language and raised it to an art.
2 **a** She participated in the creation of the Universal Declaration of Human Rights.
   b She risked her own life to help others.
3 **a** He showed bravery as a warrior and a swordsman.
   b He was a warrior and a scholar.
4 **a** This person's music was complex.
   b This composer was a talented and interesting person.

Language Focus: *Asking permission*

▸ When you want to ask permission to do something, start your sentence with these phrases.

I was wondering if / Would it be possible to / Would it be okay if . . .
I was *wondering if* *I could show a photo slideshow during my talk.*

C Listen again for these phrases and identify the teacher's decision as either true (**T**) or false (**F**).

1 It's OK to wear a medieval costume during the presentation.   T / F
2 It's OK to use the school projector to show a slideshow from a laptop.   T / F
3 It's OK to bring a sword into the classroom.   T / F
4 It's OK to play music during the presentation.   T / F

Talk It Over

Role-play with your partner. Take turns asking for permission to do various things.

> I was wondering if I could wear a costume in our next class.

> Wow, that would be great. OK!

Lesson B   *Modern heroes*

Before You Listen

 A Complete these famous quotes about genius using the words in the box. Then listen and check.

> living   born   seed   perspiration   ordinary   thunderstorms

1 *A genius can do anything except make a _____.*
   (Joey Adams, American comedian, 1911–1999)
2 *Genius is _____, not paid.* (Oscar Wilde, Irish writer, 1854–1900)
3 *To see things in the _____, that is genius.*
   (Laozi, Chinese philosopher, 6th century B.C.)
4 *Genius is one percent inspiration and ninety-nine percent _____.*
   (Thomas Edison, American inventor, 1847–1931)
5 *Genius . . . is the capacity to see ten things where the _____ man sees one.*
   (Ezra Pound, American poet, 1885–1972)
6 *Geniuses are like _____. They go against the wind, terrify people, cleanse the air.*
   (Søren Kierkegaard, Danish philosopher, 1813–1855)

B What do the quotes above mean? Discuss with a partner.

Extended Listening

 A A group of students is taking a tour of a special museum where they can hear and see images of famous people from history. Number the historical figures (**1–4**) in the order you hear them. One is not used.

a _____ Mahatma Gandhi
b _____ Thomas Jefferson
c _____ Laozi
d _____ Abraham Lincoln
e _____ Winston Churchill

B Listen again. Fill in the blanks to complete the sentences from the dialogue.

1 The best argument against democracy is a five-minute
   conversation with _____.
2 You should be the _____ you want to see in
   the world.
3 Govern a great nation as you would cook a small fish.
   Do not _____.
4 . . . your unalienable rights: _____, liberty, and the pursuit of _____.

▶ In informal conversation, we often use phrases that generally extend the category of things or ideas.

. . . or something (like that) / . . . or whatever / . . . and stuff (like that) / . . . or anything

*I enjoy camping, hiking, fishing, **and stuff like that**.*

The phrase "stuff like that" is referring to camping, hiking, fishing, and other activities like these.

 C Listen again for the modern version of the famous quotes. Match the general extender with what it refers to in the column on the right. Note: The list is not in order.

1 . . . or something like that   **a** people's rights
2 . . . or whatever   **b** govern
3 . . . and stuff like that   **c** conversation
4 . . . or anything   **d** changes you want

Catch It! Diphthong pronunciation

 A Listen to the pronunciation of these vowel combinations (diphthongs).

buy /aɪ/   boy /ɔɪ/   bow /aʊ/

 B Listen to each word and circle the vowel sound you hear.

1 /aɪ/   /ɔɪ/   /aʊ/
2 /aɪ/   /ɔɪ/   /aʊ/
3 /aɪ/   /ɔɪ/   /aʊ/
4 /aɪ/   /ɔɪ/   /aʊ/
5 /aɪ/   /ɔɪ/   /aʊ/
6 /aɪ/   /ɔɪ/   /aʊ/
7 /aɪ/   /ɔɪ/   /aʊ/

Try It Out!

Make a short list of historic figures you admire and tell your partner why you chose those people. Use your new phrases whenever you can.

Example:
A: Do you have a favorite person from history?
B: I really respect Queen Elizabeth the First.
A: Was she a great leader or something?

Globalization

10

Lesson A *The world's getting smaller!*

Warm-up

A Check the meanings of the words in **blue**. Then decide if you agree (**A**) or disagree (**D**) with each statement. Discuss your answers with a partner.

1 Most aspects of international trade benefit companies more than workers.   A / D
2 Airborne diseases are nothing serious to worry about.   A / D
3 Cultural diversity in a city is always a good thing.   A / D
4 Global warming is a natural phenomenon.   A / D
5 Globalization has more benefits than down sides.   A / D
6 Letters will still be important for correspondence 100 years from now.   A / D

B What does globalization mean to you? Discuss your ideas with a partner.

Listening

A Listen to four people talk about what globalization means to them. Circle the word or phrase which best summarizes their point.

1 **a** digital convenience   **b** business discussion
2 **a** food supplies   **b** consumption
3 **a** lower prices   **b** accessible products
4 **a** loss of cultural diversity   **b** personal weight gain

B Listen again. What is the reason they are either **for** or **against** globalization? Circle **a** or **b**.

1 **a** The GPS function on cell phones decreases personal privacy.

   b Various technologies make business communication possible.

2 **a** Globalization encourages consumption that destroys global resources.

   b Corporations encourage us to consume less than is consumed in rich countries.

3 **a** International travel will be more difficult, especially to tropical islands.

   b Products can be ordered from and delivered to people anywhere.

4 **a** The variety of products (fast food, pop music, etc.) available globally is increasing.

   b The loss of cultural variety in food, music, and clothing is unfortunate.

Further Listening

 A   Listen to four conversations about the good and bad points of globalization. Number the topics in the order you hear them.

    a   High-tech communication _____
    b   Americanization _____
    c   Information accessibility _____
    d   International travel _____

 B   Listen again. Decide if the speakers would agree (**A**) or disagree (**D**) with the statements below.

    1   Globalization targets teenagers worldwide to buy American products.   A / D
    2   Travel-related diseases are going to become more of a concern in the future.   A / D
    3   Advances in e-mail technology mean that there is no reason for letters any more.   A / D
    4   Libraries are even more important now than they used to be.   A / D

Language Focus: *Contrasting*

▸ Use these words and phrases to introduce a contrast:

but / however / on the other hand / on the contrary

*Globalization is supported by millions of consumers and international corporations; **however**, there are also millions of people who are against it.*

 C   Listen again for the contrasting phrases and choose which sentence best summarizes the **contrasting** point. Circle **a** or **b**.

    1   **a** Corporations will become richer as globalization promotes democracy worldwide.
        b Globalization could be used to spread democracy, rather than just selling American brands.
    2   **a** International travel has contributed to the spread of disease.
        b Globalization is preventing problems in global health.
    3   **a** Even grandmothers enjoy sending text messages from their cell phones.
        b Electronic communication is missing the human touch of tradition.
    4   **a** There's so much information available on the Internet, it's difficult to choose what to read.
        b Reading Internet information on a computer screen is not as useful as reading library books.

Talk It Over

Talk with your partner about globalization. Use your new phrases for contrasting.

> The Internet is educational.

> Yeah. On the other hand, it can be unreliable.

Lesson B *The rich get richer . . .*

Before You Listen

 A Match the words and phrases that you will hear in this lesson with their definitions. Listen and check.

1 The World Bank
2 wealth inequality
3 Third World debt
4 The World Trade Organization
5 privatization

a borrowed money that developing countries must pay back
b giving control of a public resource or service to a company
c an organization that makes rules about trade between countries
d the gap between rich and poor people
e an organization that loans money to help poor countries

B Complete the summary below using the words and phrases in the box. Listen and check.

enormous   exploits   infrastructure   outsourcing   pocket (*v.*)   standard of living

Some people believe that _____ jobs to a foreign country hurts workers in the home country. It also _____ workers in the foreign country because companies pay them a low wage and _____ a high profit. However, others say there is an _____ benefit for the foreign country. The company improves the local _____ (for example, electricity and water systems) and the money that workers earn raises their _____.

Extended Listening

 A Two experts of international politics debate live on the podcast news program *Global Hope*. What topics are raised? Number them in the order you hear them.

a privatization   _____
b standard of living   _____
c wealth inequality   _____
d global poverty   _____
e economic growth   _____
f outsourcing jobs   _____
g international trade   _____

B Listen again. Who supports which actions? Check the box.

	Heather	Sheldon
1 Outsourcing U.S. jobs to developing countries		
2 Protecting workers in developing countries		
3 Corporate solutions to the problems of poverty		
4 Free trade		
5 Fair trade		
6 Privatization of public resources		
7 Forgiving debt of poor countries		

▶ We use these phrases when we want to stop other people from interrupting us.

Please, let me finish / Excuse me, I'm not quite done / I'm not done yet / Permit me to finish

 C Listen for the phrases that the speakers use to stop the other person from interrupting them. Then, connect the phrase on the left with the point the speaker is trying to make.

1 Please, I'm not finished yet . . .
2 Excuse me, I'm not quite done here . . .
3 Please, let me finish . . .
4 Permit me . . .

a Paying back World Bank loans means there is no money left to help people.
b Owners pocket profits at the workers' expense.
c Some companies create a better quality of life for workers while improving their standard of living.
d Privatization concentrates wealth in the hands of a few people.

Catch It! Intrusion

 A Sometimes extra sounds appear between spoken words to make them easier for us to say quickly. Look at the following examples.

The /r/ sound in the expression *law and order* ▶ law$_r$ and order
The /w/ sound between the words *no* and *entry* ▶ no $_w$entry
The /y/ sound between the words *be* and *early* ▶ be $_y$early

 B Listen and decide which sounds you hear between the words. Write **r**, **w**, or **y** between the words.

1 I am going now.
2 Visiting the spa is a good idea.
3 Sorry, no apples today.
4 I agree with you.
5 Just do it.
6 What will she offer?

Try It Out!

Discuss the causes, effects, and solutions of poverty in small groups. Use your conversation strategies to keep talking if someone interrupts you.

Example:
A: It makes sense to cancel Third World debt because . . .
B: No, I don't think . . .
A: Please, let me finish . . . because the real value of the debt actually isn't very much.

Earth's Resources

11

Lesson A   *It's a major concern.*

Warm-up

A   Complete the paragraph below, using the words in the box. Two items are extra. Then listen and check.

> crisis   regulations   efficient   sanitation   glaciers   commodification
>
> precious   consumption   emissions   deforestation   erosion   conservation

There are a lot of problems with the world's environment today. Global warming causes

1. _____ to melt, so we lose fresh water to the ocean. Before the **2.** _____ becomes

more serious, we need to think about our **3.** _____ of resources. We really need to become

more **4.** _____ in our water usage. Governments also need to pass **5.** _____ about

gas **6.** _____. We need to plant more trees to undo the damage caused by

7. _____. Too many people living in one place has caused soil **8.** _____. The time

to think about the **9.** _____ of **10.** _____ global resources is now!

B   What about you? What is your opinion about the need for conservation? Discuss with a partner.

Listening

A   Listen to four experts talk about the problems of food and water. Match the expert's field with the issue they describe.

1 economist	**a** water shortage
2 scientist	**b** water commodification
3 farmer	**c** food distribution
4 government worker	**d** food shortage

B   What is the main message of each speaker? Circle **a** or **b**.

1   **a**   Companies can't solve food problems with free trade.

    b   The food crisis is the result of government regulation.

2   **a**   Global demand for drinking water is greater than the supply.

    b   Two-thirds of the population needs more access to fresh water today.

3   **a**   The world is running out of land to grow food because of overpopulation.

    b   In the future, it will be possible to produce enough food to feed everyone.

4   **a**   Fresh drinking water is a very important resource.

    b   The government cannot prevent commodification.

Further Listening

A Listen to a question and answer session between an expert panel and an audience. What topics do they address? Number them in the order you hear them.

a Causes of and solutions to water shortage _____

b Environmental impact of eating beef _____

c Uses of fresh water _____

d Not using the land properly _____

B Listen again and decide whether the following statements are true (**T**) or false (**F**), according to the speakers. Circle your answer.

1	The speaker's friends have stopped eating beef because it's unhealthy.	T / F
2	Raising cows requires land that could be better used for planting rice or wheat.	T / F
3	Some problems with soil are caused naturally by rain and changes in the weather.	T / F
4	Humans have damaged the soil through deforestation.	T / F
5	Overpopulation is the main reason glaciers melt and rivers dry up.	T / F
6	Desalination of sea water is the best solution for the water crisis.	T / F
7	The computer industry uses a lot of water to make silicon chips.	T / F
8	Bottled water is generally healthier than tap water.	T / F

Language Focus: *Prefacing concerns*

▶ You can use these phrases to introduce your points of concern.

probably the least important is . . . / one of my concerns is . . . / the biggest problem might be . . . / a major concern is . . .

A: I'd like to go skiing but the biggest problem might be finding the money to get there.

B: One of my concerns about skiing is falling and hurting myself.

C Listen for the phrases that preface concern and match the concerns.

1 The biggest problem might be . . .   a there's a problem of using land the wrong way.

2 One of my concerns is . . .   b desalination, changing sea water into fresh water.

3 Probably the least important is . . .   c cows releasing methane gas into the atmosphere.

4 My major concern is . . .   d water use in agriculture.

Talk It Over

Talk with a partner about problems concerning land and water. Use your new phrases when you need them.

> In the future, the population will grow. One of my concerns is that there won't be enough drinking water for everyone.

> Fresh water is important, not just for drinking, but for farming, too.

Lesson B *We're running out!*

Before You Listen

A Look at the list of items below. Decide whether each item is most likely to be used when talking about water (**W**), oil (**O**), or soil (**S**)? Write **W**, **O**, or **S** next to each item.

1 _____ fertile
2 _____ drive up the prices
3 _____ supply and demand
4 _____ nutrients
5 _____ waste
6 _____ sewage treatment plant

B Read the sentences below. Do you agree (**A**) or disagree (**D**)? Share your answers with a partner.

1 I would use my bicycle or public transportation if it would help the environment.   A / D
2 Drinking water will soon become more valuable than oil throughout the world.   A / D
3 My country has many laws to stop companies from harming the environment.   A / D
4 If my community organized a group to plant more trees, I might join them.   A / D

Extended Listening

  A Listen to three students preparing for a team presentation on issues concerning global resources. Match the resource with the main problem that the students talk about. Two problems are not used.

1 Oil
2 Soil
3 Water

a damage from weather
b increase in price
c increasingly difficult to get to
d not enough
e losing its quality

  B Listen again. Complete the statements below.

1 **Fact:** The Earth _____ running out of oil.
2 **Fact:** Much of the world's oil is _____ underground or under _____.
3 **Fact:** Farming is done on only _____ percent of the land on Earth.
4 **Fact:** To improve soil, we have to _____ and plow more carefully.
5 **Fact:** Commercial bottled water is less _____ than public water supplies.

Conversation Strategy: *Tripling your reaction*

▶ To show our enthusiasm, we sometimes react by repeating the same word a few times, or we use a few words that are similar in meaning.

yeah, yeah, yeah / right, right, right / yeah, right, exactly / good, great, wonderful

A: People don't really understand how important it is to conserve water.

B: Yeah, right, exactly!

 C Listen again for the tripled reactions and number them in the order you hear them.

a Good, great, wonderful _____
b Right, right, right _____
c Sure, yeah, right _____
d Yeah, yeah, yeah _____

Catch It! Distinguishing vowels

 A Some vowel sounds are quite similar, especially when spoken quickly, like *fine/fun* or *hungry/angry*. Listen carefully to the following response and decide which question or statement it matches. Circle **a** or **b**.

Response: Don't touch that bug!
Question: **a** Will it bite me?
b What's inside it?

 B Listen especially to the final word or phrase in the spoken response and choose **a** or **b** as the correct match.

1 a It will grow bigger.   **b** It moves fast on the ocean.
2 a Are the leaves very beautiful?   **b** Will it take long to read?
3 a Oh, it took so long.   **b** Oh, it was very high.
4 a It's delicious.   **b** It's too low.
5 a Yes, he wanted some exercise.   **b** Yes, he has to finish a project.
6 a That's right, we're finished.   **b** Yes. Someone should clean it up.

Try It Out!

Can you think of any other problems, effects, or solutions concerning global resources? Tell your partner. When you listen to your partner's ideas, use your new conversation strategy to react.

A: One major concern I have is how much plastic packaging we use.
B: Right, right, right!

Discovery

Lesson A — Solutions to global problems

Warm-up

 A Match the words and phrases you will hear in this lesson with their definitions. Listen and check.

1	bio-fuels	a	fair treatment of and equal benefits for all people
2	tidal energy	b	dishonest use of power for personal gain
3	aerodynamics	c	natural energy from plants, like corn
4	endangered species	d	study of things moving in the air
5	social justice	e	person who has left his or her country to avoid danger
6	corruption	f	plants or animals that may become extinct
7	refugee	g	natural power of the ocean waves

B Discuss with a partner. Which of the topics or issues listed above are you interested in? Why?

Listening

 A Listen to four people talk about their hopes for discoveries in various fields. Number the fields they talk about in the order you hear them.

 B What specific point does each speaker make? Choose **a** or **b** and circle your answer.

1 **a** Robots are better than humans at caring for the elderly.
  b Robots may be necessary to do the work of younger people in an aging society.

2 **a** Bio-fuels are a good solution to the problem of supplying energy.
  b Tidal power is a better source of alternative energy.

3 **a** Social justice means protecting the rights of the individual.
  b Preventing corruption is the goal that all justice issues depend upon.

4 **a** Products created in a zero-gravity environment are important and valuable.
  b Industry depends on government tax money to fund space stations.

Further Listening

 A   Listen to a question-and-answer session as listeners call in to a radio talk-show. What topics do they address? Number them (**1–4**) in the order you hear them.

a Preventing war   _____

b Helping people   _____

c Preserving the ecosystem   _____

d Dealing with global warming _____

 B   Listen again and decide whether the following statements are true (**T**) or false (**F**), according to the speakers. Circle your answer.

1 All governments are cooperating with laws to reduce greenhouse gas emissions.   T / F

2 It's possible to clean up polluted rivers.   T / F

3 If we could control the arms trade, we might stop more wars.   T / F

4 The speakers are pessimistic about finding solutions to today's problems.   T / F

Language Focus: *Emphasizing*

▸ **We use these words and phrases to introduce a point that we want to emphasize strongly.**

primarily / mainly / especially / particularly / above all

*I'd like to talk about solutions to global problems, **above all**, alternative energy sources.*

C   Listen for the phrases that introduce emphasis and choose the point that's being emphasized. Circle **a** or **b**.

1 **Primarily:** Reducing global warming is difficult because some governments . . .

    a build too many office buildings.

    b won't pass laws to reduce greenhouse gas emissions.

2 **Mainly:** We can solve the ecosystem problem by . . .

    a cleaning our polluted waters.

    b making fishing illegal.

3 **Particularly:** The way to stop war is to give an organization like the United Nations the power to . . .

    a make nuclear weapons illegal.

    b prevent conflicts.

4 **Above all:** We need to keep people alive by . . .

    a feeding the hungry and treating the sick.

    b giving them houses and cars.

Talk It Over

Talk with a partner about world problems that you would like to see solved. Use your new phrases when you need them.

> What can we do to stop global warming?

> Above all, we should conserve energy.

Lesson B   *Welcome to the future!*

Before You Listen

A   Are advances in some areas more important than others? Look at the list below and use a dictionary to check the meaning of any word you don't know. Then decide where you think research and investment is most needed from **5** (most urgent) to **1** (least urgent).

1   space exploration   5   4   3   2   1
2   health and disease   5   4   3   2   1
3   robotics   5   4   3   2   1
4   environment   5   4   3   2   1
5   cryogenics   5   4   3   2   1

B   Read the sentences. Do you agree (**A**) or disagree (**D**) with them? Compare your answers with a partner.

1   We can solve most of the global problems we face today.   A / D
2   I believe in peoples' ability to make good decisions.   A / D
3   Most politicians are more interested in themselves than in the future of the world.   A / D
4   Human beings are basically too selfish to change.   A / D

Extended Listening

A   A man from today is waking up in the year 2525. He learns that humans have discovered solutions to many global problems. Which problems does he ask about? Listen and number them in the order you hear them. Two are not used.

a   war   _____
b   environment   _____
c   disease   _____
d   energy   _____
e   poverty   _____

B   Listen again. How was each problem solved? Circle **a**, **b**, or **c**.

1   **a** They did animal research and discovered how to stop diseases.

    b They created new medicines to stop diseases.

    c They worked with human DNA and discovered how to stop diseases.

2   **a** There are no more wars because the world leaders were women.

    b There are no more wars because all countries were combined into one country.

    c There are no more wars because there are 615 states.

3   **a** There are no more resources so there's no more poverty.

    b Everything that people need is provided to them, so there's no more poverty.

    c People are kind now, so there's no more poverty.

Conversation Strategy: *Changing the word*

▸ We sometimes use a different word with the same or a similar meaning to add variety or to show agreement in a conversation or discussion.

A: We have to do something about **global warming**.
B: Yeah, those **greenhouse gases**.
A: Right!

 C Listen again for the changed words or phrases and fill in the blanks below.

a Took very little _____ / happened quite _____

b Remarkable / un_____

c Naturally / of _____

d Unnecessary / no _____

Catch It! Reported speech

 A Reported (or indirect) speech usually tells us what someone has said. Look at the two sentences below. In the first one, the exact words of the speaker are quoted. The second one uses reported speech to report the speaker's words. Listen and notice the difference in intonation.

Direct speech: Did he say, "What's going on here?"
Reported speech: Did he ask what's been going on here?

 B Listen and decide whether these sentences use direct speech (**DS**) or reported speech (**RS**).

1 DS / RS	**3** DS / RS	**5** DS / RS	**7** DS / RS
2 DS / RS	**4** DS / RS	**6** DS / RS	

Try It Out!

Can you think of any other discoveries of the future that will make our lives and the world better? Work with a partner and share your views. When you listen to your partner, try to use a different word with a similar meaning in your response.

A: I think it would be really interesting if they discovered life on another planet.
B: Oh, fascinating, yes. Wonderful!

Practice Test

Part 1

For each question, you will see a photograph and hear four short sentences. You will not see the sentences in writing, so you must listen carefully. The sentences will be spoken one time only. Choose the sentence that best describes what you see in the photo. Each question is two points.

1   a   b   c   d

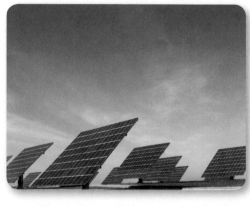

2   a   b   c   d

3   a   b   c   d

4 a b c d

5 a b c d

6 a b c d

Part 2

For each question, you will hear a question or statement and three responses. You will not see the question or responses in writing, so you must listen carefully. They will be spoken one time only. Choose the best response to the question or statement.

7   a   b   c

8   a   b   c

9   a   b   c

10   a   b   c

11   a   b   c

12   a   b   c

13   a   b   c

Part 3

You will hear two conversations. Listen to each conversation, and choose the best response to each question. You will not see the conversations in writing, so you must listen carefully. You will hear each conversation one time only.

Conversation 1

14 What has their company been doing in developing countries?
   a working to improve their corporate image
   b controlling water resources for profit
   c marketing different styles of bottled water
   d working on a water recommendation report

15 Why is the woman against water commodification?
   a She is worried about her personal image.
   b She knows bottled water sales in developing countries are falling.
   c She thinks the poor people will fight against the company.
   d She believes that water is a human right.

16 What is the man's proposed solution?
   a Focus on increasing sales of bottled water in developed countries.
   b Find new markets for bottled water.
   c Ask the board of directors for more money for research.
   d Ask the marketing department to change the water packaging.

Conversation 2

17 Who would likely listen to this talk?
   a doctors and medical personnel
   b government workers
   c humanitarian aid volunteers
   d tourists to Africa

18 What is NOT true about malaria?
   a Every year a million people around the world die from the disease.
   b Mosquito nets containing insecticide can help prevent the disease.
   c Ninety percent of malaria deaths occur in Africa.
   d Education is the key to prevention.

19 According to the speaker, which of these statements about the AIDS problem in Africa is true?
   a Millions of people are dying from it every day.
   b No one cares about HIV-positive people and their families.
   c The majority of the world's HIV patients live in Africa.
   d AIDS education has generally been unsuccessful.

Part 4

You will hear two short talks. Listen to each talk, and choose the best response to each question. You will not see the talks in writing, so you must listen carefully. You will hear each talk one time only.

Talk 1

20 What examples of biofuels does the speaker mention?
    a gas and oil   **b** rice and wheat
    c sugar and corn   **d** insects and termites

21 Why is biofuel production a problem?
    a It increases our dependence on fossil fuels.
    b It uses land that can be better used to farm other crops.
    c It leads to an increase in pests, such as termites.
    d It produces a lot of chemicals.

22 What did researchers discover that might help biofuel production?
    a Sugar and corn could possibly replace wood and grass as biofuels.
    b The wood-eating termite is an insect with three stomachs.
    c A chemical from termites could be used to produce fuel.
    d Governments are urging farmers to grow biofuel crops.

Talk 2

23 What is the problem described by the speaker?
    a Over a billion people do not have enough fresh drinking water.
    b Diseases and bacteria in the water kill millions of people every day.
    c People in rich countries take their clean drinking water for granted.
    d Clean, bottled water is expensive to transport to rural villages.

24 Which statement about The WaterTube is true?
    a It takes two people to carry it.
    b It requires electricity or batteries.
    c It can be used for one year.
    d It's quite expensive.

25 What does the speaker's organization intend to do?
    a sell the WaterTube to every person who needs one
    b sell the WaterTube to governments that will sell them in villages
    c use the WaterTube to destroy bacteria globally
    d give the WaterTube free to every person who needs one

Practice Test 2 Answer Sheet

Part 1

1 ⓐ ⓑ ⓒ ⓓ   4 ⓐ ⓑ ⓒ ⓓ

2 ⓐ ⓑ ⓒ ⓓ   5 ⓐ ⓑ ⓒ ⓓ

3 ⓐ ⓑ ⓒ ⓓ   6 ⓐ ⓑ ⓒ ⓓ

Part 2

7 ⓐ ⓑ ⓒ   11 ⓐ ⓑ ⓒ

8 ⓐ ⓑ ⓒ   12 ⓐ ⓑ ⓒ

9 ⓐ ⓑ ⓒ   13 ⓐ ⓑ ⓒ

10 ⓐ ⓑ ⓒ

Part 3

14 ⓐ ⓑ ⓒ ⓓ   17 ⓐ ⓑ ⓒ ⓓ

15 ⓐ ⓑ ⓒ ⓓ   18 ⓐ ⓑ ⓒ ⓓ

16 ⓐ ⓑ ⓒ ⓓ   19 ⓐ ⓑ ⓒ ⓓ

Part 4

20 ⓐ ⓑ ⓒ ⓓ   23 ⓐ ⓑ ⓒ ⓓ

21 ⓐ ⓑ ⓒ ⓓ   24 ⓐ ⓑ ⓒ ⓓ

22 ⓐ ⓑ ⓒ ⓓ   25 ⓐ ⓑ ⓒ ⓓ

Introduction to the Self-Study Units

Everyone needs more listening practice. So, after you finish each unit, go to the self-study section. Listen to the CD in the back of the book and take the 10-point quiz.

Write your answers on the side of the page.

The CD is yours, so listen as many times as you want!

Good luck!!

Self-Study

TRACK
1

For each question, you will see a photograph and hear four short sentences. You will not see the sentences in writing, so you must listen carefully. The sentences will be spoken one time only. Choose the sentence that best describes what you see in the photo. Each question is two points.

Total ____

1 a   b   c   d

2 a   b   c   d

1 ___

2 ___

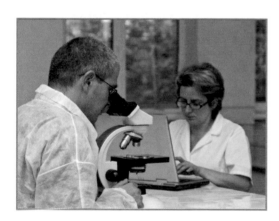

3 a   b   c   d

4 a   b   c   d

3 ___

4 ___

5 a   b   c   d

5 ___

Self-Study

Total _____

TRACK
2

For each question, you will hear a question or statement and three responses. You will not see the question or responses in writing, so you must listen carefully. They will be spoken one time only. Choose the best response to the question or statement.

1 ___

2 ___

3 ___

4 ___

5 ___

6 ___

7 ___

8 ___

9 ___

10 ___

1	a	b	c
2	a	b	c
3	a	b	c
4	a	b	c
5	a	b	c
6	a	b	c
7	a	b	c
8	a	b	c
9	a	b	c
10	a	b	c

Self-Study

TRACK
3

You will hear two conversations. Listen to each conversation, and choose the best response to each question. You will not see the conversations in writing, so you must listen carefully. You will hear each conversation one time only. Each question is worth two points.

Total _____

Conversation 1

1 What will happen soon?

   a They will prepare for a meeting with the president.

   b Some workers at the company will be fired.

   c The company will celebrate its sales.

   d The president will be coming.

1 ___

2 Who is the woman's friend?

   a the sales director   **c** the president

   b the secretary   **d** the vice-president

2 ___

Conversation 2

3 What are the speakers discussing?

   a a company friend   **c** global competition

   b a job vacancy   **d** the recession

3 ___

4 Why can't the man give the woman a job?

   a Her resume is too good for the position.

   b He already gave the job to her friend.

   c There is no opening for the position she wants.

   d There is a high turnover of staff.

4 ___

5 What is the woman's attitude?

   a She is happy to be considered for the position in the future.

   b She is angry at her friend for giving her bad information.

   c She is interested in taking a lower position at the company.

   d She is flexible about health insurance.

5 ___

Self-Study

Total ___

TRACK
4

You will hear two talks. Listen to each speaker and choose the best response to each question. You will not see the talks in writing, so you must listen carefully. You will hear each speaker one time only. Each question is worth two points.

Recording 1 (a message)

1 ___

1   Why is the speaker calling?

    a to say she misses him at work

    b to apologize for the messages

    c to ask about pictures on the wall of his office

    d to invite him to go with her this weekend

2 ___

2   What is their relationship?

    a close friends   **c** co-workers

    b relatives   **d** boyfriend and girlfriend

Recording 2 (an announcement)

3 ___

3   What kind of place is described in the advertisement?

    a a shopping mall   **c** a restaurant

    b a gourmet building **d** a cooking school

4 ___

4   Where is the best place for busy people to eat?

    a on the first floor   **c** on the top floor

    b on the second floor **d** in the cooking school

5 ___

5   What are customers NOT able to do there?

    a learn to cook   **c** bring food from home

    b receive recipes   **d** enjoy the view

Self-Study

TRACK
5

For each question, you will see a photograph and hear four short sentences. You will not see the sentences in writing, so you must listen carefully. The sentences will be spoken one time only. Choose the sentence that best describes what you see in the photo. Each question is two points.

Total _____

1 a   b   c   d

2 a   b   c   d

1 ___

2 ___

3 a   b   c   d

4 a   b   c   d

3 ___

4 ___

5 a   b   c   d

5 ___

Self-Study

Total ____

TRACK
6

For each question, you will hear a question or statement, and three responses. You will not see the question or responses in writing, so you must listen carefully. They will be spoken one time only. Choose the best response to the question or statement.

1 ___

2 ___

3 ___

4 ___

5 ___

6 ___

7 ___

8 ___

9 ___

10 ___

1   a   b   c

2   a   b   c

3   a   b   c

4   a   b   c

5   a   b   c

6   a   b   c

7   a   b   c

8   a   b   c

9   a   b   c

10   a   b   c

Self-Study

TRACK
7

You will hear two conversations. Listen to each conversation, and choose the best response to each question. You will not see the conversations in writing, so you must listen carefully. You will hear each conversation one time only. Each question is worth two points.

Total _____

Conversation 1

1 What is the man's situation?

   a He broke his engagement with his fiancée.

   b He wants a date with the woman.

   c He had conflict issues with his ex-fiancée.

   d He had nothing in common with his ex-fiancée.

1 ___

2 What did the man's ex-fiancée use to do?

   a give him compliments   **c** yell and fight dramatically

   b discuss past issues calmly   **d** throw things at him

2 ___

Conversation 2

3 What are the speakers talking about?

   a Simon's reaction   **c** Simon's fiancée's sister

   b the woman's new job   **d** the new travel agency downstairs

3 ___

4 Who is going to be surprised?

   a Simon   **c** Simon's sister

   b Simon's fiancée   **d** the woman's boyfriend

4 ___

5 What is the big surprise?

   a Simon is dating his fiancée's sister.

   b Simon is planning a special trip.

   c Simon is getting engaged.

   d Simon is buying an island.

5 ___

Self-Study

Total _____

TRACK
8

For each question, you will hear a question or statement, and three responses. You will not see the question or responses in writing, so you must listen carefully. They will be spoken one time only. Choose the best response to the question or statement.

1 ___

2 ___

3 ___

4 ___

5 ___

6 ___

7 ___

8 ___

9 ___

10 ___

1   a   b   c

2   a   b   c

3   a   b   c

4   a   b   c

5   a   b   c

6   a   b   c

7   a   b   c

8   a   b   c

9   a   b   c

10   a   b   c

You will hear two talks. Listen to each speaker, and choose the best response to each question. You will not see the talks in writing, so you must listen carefully. You will hear each speaker one time only. Each question is worth two points.

Total ____

Talk 1

1 How does the speaker feel about U.S. history?

a She feels it is unimportant.

b She thinks it should focus only on women.

c She thinks it focuses on the wrong types of women.

d She feels that men are better at studying history.

1 ___

2 Why does the speaker think that U.S. history books should teach about Ida B. Wells and Emma Goldman?

a Because they are the most important female historical figures.

b Because they were both African-Americans.

c Because they represent the strength of the American character.

d Because they were critical of the U.S. government.

2 ___

Talk 2

3 What is the main point of this talk?

a To tell the purpose of learning history.

b To explain the history of education.

c To present a new approach to history education.

d To criticize students' history study habits.

3 ___

4 How can students see history as a "cause-and-effect" relationship?

a By asking questions about the future.

b By studying in the traditional method.

c By looking for answers to present-day problems.

d By memorizing historical facts.

4 ___

5 Why do education critics say that only memorizing historical facts is a waste of time?

a Because students are not good at memorizing names, places, and dates.

b Because students don't like memorizing names, places, and dates.

c Because memorizing questions is more important.

d Because memorizing is just a part of understanding the answers to questions

5 ___

Total ____

TRACK
10

For each question, you will hear a question or statement, and three responses. You will not see the question or responses in writing, so you must listen carefully. They will be spoken one time only. Choose the best response to the question or statement.

1 ___

1 a b c

2 ___

2 a b c

3 ___

3 a b c

4 ___

4 a b c

5 ___

5 a b c

6 ___

6 a b c

7 ___

7 a b c

8 ___

8 a b c

9 ___

9 a b c

10 ___

10 a b c

TRACK
11

You will hear two conversations. Listen to each conversation, and choose the best response to each question. You will not see the conversations in writing, so you must listen carefully. You will hear each conversation one time only. Each question is worth two points.

Total ____

Conversation 1

1 What is the main topic of their conversation?

    a the rise in ocean levels   **c** the decrease of farm land

    b the effects of global warming   **d** the best source of energy

1 ____

2 Which kind of energy is NOT mentioned as a renewable resource?

    a the sun   **c** ocean tides

    b land use   **d** the wind

2 ____

Conversation 2

3 What is the main point of their conversation?

    a Global warming is real.

    b Water conservation is necessary.

    c Desalinization is damaging to the environment.

    d The global population is increasing.

3 ____

4 Which of the following is NOT mentioned by the woman as a water problem?

    a Global warming dries up fresh water sources, like lakes.

    b Processing salt water into drinking water causes pollution.

    c We need water for growing food.

    d There's not enough water to feed farm animals.

4 ____

5 How much of the Earth's water will be available for drinking in the future?

    a less than 2%   **c** more than 2%

    b 2%   **d** The speaker doesn't say.

5 ____

Total ___

TRACK
12

You will hear two talks. Listen to each speaker, and choose the best response to each question. You will not see the talks in writing, so you must listen carefully. You will hear each speaker one time only. Each question is worth two points.

Talk 1

1 ___

1 What is the speaker's main point?

    a Education needs to be improved.

    b The world's economy is in terrible condition.

    c "Discovery" is not limited only to science.

    d Great thinkers have answered many questions.

2 ___

2 Which field is NOT mentioned as an area for discovery?

    a economics   **c** government

    b chemistry   **d** education

Talk 2

3 ___

3 What is the main point of the talk?

    a We are not alone in the universe.

    b Finding alien life would be a great discovery.

    c Experts need money for more research.

    d Aliens would have advanced technology.

4 ___

4 What would be a benefit of contact with an alien civilization?

    a They would see how advanced we were.

    b We would see that they are not destructive monsters.

    c We could share our scientific knowledge with them.

    d They could share different kinds of knowledge with us.

5 ___

5 What should we do if we want to discover aliens?

    a send a message into space   **c** look for alien spaceships

    b listen for their messages from space   **d** travel into space